minimal

INTERIORS

ROCKPORT

minimal

INTERIORS

GLOUCESTER MASSACHUSETTS

ROCKPORT

PUBLISHERS

Ann McArdle

First published in the United States of America by
Rockport Publishers, Inc.
33 Commercial Street
Gloucester, Massachusetts 01930-5089
Telephone: (978) 282-9590
Facsimile: (978) 283-2742
www.rockpub.com

ISBN 1-56496-612-7

10 9 8 7 6 5 4 3 2

Design: Sawyer Design Associates, Inc.

Front Cover Images

Top:	Peter Forbes and Associates (Photo: Nick Wheeler Photographers)
Bottom Left:	Photo Courtesy of Cassina USA
Bottom Center:	Wally Cunningham (Photo: Tim Street-Porter)
Bottom Right:	Paolo Piva (Photo: Courtesy of B&B Italia)

Back Cover Images

Top:	Antoine Kripacz (Photo: Tim-Street-Porter)
Center:	Edardo Souto Mora (Photo: Luis Ferreira Alves)
Bottom:	Barbara Barry (Photo: Tim Street-Porter)

Printed in China.

contents

introduction

Minimalism is the reduction of a design to its essence, intensifying the impact of its inherent beauty. This standard is used to create beauty within the home by presenting the space without excessive ornamentation. Emphasis is on the careful placement of furnishings and select accessories. Limiting the use of decorative accents allows the eye to roam, to appreciate the space itself as a visual resting place. Let the activity that takes place in a room be its centerpiece, and provide only the necessary tools for that activity.

The subtlety of the design sets free the spirit of the room and its occupants.

Apply the principles of minimalism to create a cohesively seductive atmosphere. But don't worry about adhering strictly to their principles; you can incorporate aspects of the style into any home. This book features examples of minimal decor that range from bare essence to a more decorated look within the minimalist aesthetic. The emphasis is on moderation and purity of form. Contemporary architecture and furnishings lend themselves to the look, but minimalism also can be achieved in more classic spaces, or with classic elements.

Start with the basics—the space and its boundaries and the necessary furniture. Choose a color scheme to suit your taste—monochromatic, unassuming pale tones, or dramatic, bold hues. Arrange furniture for utility and effect. Large pieces set away from a wall appear to float in the space. The absence of surrounding elements gives favorite accessories weight and life. Select lighting fixtures of unobtrusive color or size, such as tiny halogens strung on wires suspended from the ceiling, or opt for ones that are invisible, recessed into walls or ceilings. Add accent lighting to articulate and dramatize the sculptural quality of fabrics, artifacts, and architectural elements.

Take cues from the empty room. The architectural elements will indicate its treatments; your style will define the environment within it.

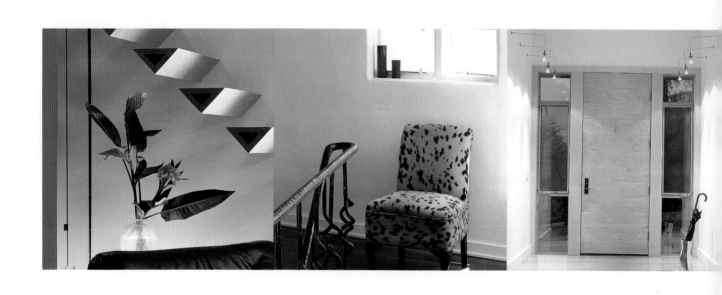

entrances

Draw guests into your home with accent lighting on a

single sculpture at the end of an entrance hall. Here,

open architecture inspires the gallery treatment.

Photo: Douglas A. Salin
Lighting Design: Linda Ferry, IES, ASID Affiliate
Architecture: David Allen Smith

Turn your stairway into sculpture on a grand scale by

placing lighting under the nosing of the steps.

Architectural detail that speaks for itself is a hallmark

of minimalism.

Photo: Robert Ames Cook
Lighting Design: Craig Roeder, IALD
Design: Loyd Ray Taylor and Charles Paxton Gremillion
Architecture: Hendricks and Wall

An entrance of mullioned glass sets the decor in

motion, allowing for the interplay of light and shadow.

A single accessory is all that is needed here.

Photo: Tim Street-Porter
Design: Josh Schweitzer, Schweitzer BIM

In an entryway with level changes, use beautiful wood flooring as an ornament. A contrasting wood step adds interest and concentrates appropriately draws attention to itself.

Photo: Luis Ferreira Alves
Architecture: Souto Moura

Contemporary architecture can be its own decor; adornments would only distract from the intriguing form of this stairway area. The playful effect of the light gives life to the stark structural lines.

Photo: Tim Street-Porter
Design: Wally Cunningham, Architect

This stairway is reduced to its functional essence. Its cantilevered treads are seemingly suspended in air. Use the sparest contemporary furnishings to enhance a serene space such as this one.

Photo: Peter Paige
Design: Damga Design

Clean, well-lit surfaces create a pleasing entrance. Here,

the architectural lines and unadorned space concentrate

attention on the door, whose function is the raison

d'être of the entryway.

Photo: John Sutton
Design: Dan Phipps and Associates

A minimal look can be achieved in a space not obviously

suited for it. Here, the shiny floor surface is a foil for the

hammered and twisted balustrade. Undressed windows

and a lone armless chair work together in understated

harmony.

Photo: Tim Street-Porter
Design: Brian Murphy Architects

A stylized stairway gains interest from a black-and-natural-wood color scheme. String unobtrusive halogen lamps on a floor-to-ceiling wire to radiate light without adding mass.

Photo: Luis Gordoa
Architecture: Kalach + Alvarez

Create interest in an entryway with a shoji-like window wall. Bare floors and interior walls provide no distraction.

Photo: Luis Ferreira Alves
Architecture: Souto Moura

Create a smooth wall surface with flat panel doors and concealed hardware to hide useful storage space in an entryway. Stain the doors in a silver tone to complement a metal table and chairs, keeping the look spare and unified.

Photo: Tim Street-Porter
Design: Terron Schaeffer

living rooms

To bring the focus inside a room, close retractable shoji screens, creating textural interest and adding a warm glow to the spare look.

Photo: Christopher Dow
Architecture: Steven Ehrlich

Decorate to enhance panoramic views of the exterior landscape. Light colors, clean lines, and a glass-topped table unite toward this end.

Photo: Christopher Dow
Architecture: Steven Ehrlich

Bright-red contemporary sectional seating is the center-piece of this spare living room. Built-in cabinets hide clutter. Set lighting unobtrusively above; leave windows bare to provide a view and allow daylight in. Add a dark coffee table to anchor a vigorous, functional scheme.

Photo: Russell Abraham
Design: Swatt and Stein Architects

The fireplace and pillars create architectural interest in
this open living space. Use neutral tones to provide a
soothing backdrop for color and texture introduced in
custom shelving.

Design: Michael C.F. Chan & Associates, Inc.

Keep lines and furnishings spare when introducing bold, contrasting colors. Here, wood floors and flat-front cabinets of similar hue combined with the wall treatment make for a quiet backdrop.

Photo: Russell Abraham
Design: Swatt Architects

Carefully select bold animal prints to use in an

otherwise unadorned space. A lone contemporary

chaise provides definition in this black-and-white room.

Photo: Tom Bonner
Architecture: Central Office of Architecture Partners

Let a windowed wall leading to the patio dictate your

decor. Coordinate black leather contemporary furniture

with black trim to define the space. Light walls and

floor contribute to the contemplative mood.

Photo: Tom Bonner
Architecture: Central Office of Architecture Partners

Place bulkier pieces at the inner extremities of a living room where heavy posts add density. Continue the flow of walls and floors toward the windows and patio beyond by using low furnishings that do not obstruct the view. A glass coffee table adds utility without distraction.

Photo: Fernando Cordero
Architecture: Kalach and Alvarez

Choose a central piece of furniture that has an airy quality, such as this unique seating arrangement, to simplify the tone of a room full of decorative accents.

Photo: Salvatore M. Lovinello
Design: David A. Seglin, HSP/Ltd. Seglin Associates

Let pale hardwood floors brighten an imposing room that has a dark ceiling. Simple furnishings and carefully chosen artwork provide a peaceful, Asian ambiance.

Photo: Richard Mandelkorn
Design: Celeste Cooper

Achieve the stripped-down look of an art gallery with

bare hardwood floors, solid shutters, and light-colored

walls and furnishings. Accent lighting on artwork

completes the effect.

Photo: Stephen Fridge
Lighting Design: Randall Whitehead
Design: Kent Wright

Heighten the visual impact of a spectacular inlaid

wood floor with transparent and semitransparent

dining furniture. Allow the pattern of the floor to

dictate placement of furnishings for optimal effect.

Photo: Kentucky Wood Floors
Floor Design: Suzan Santiago

For a living room with architectural interest, choose restrained furnishings to heighten the impact of the room itself. A chair such as this one, at once unobtrusive and stylish, punctuates rather than overwhelms the space.

Photo: ©Richard Bryant/Arcaid
Architecture: Gwathmey Siegel and Associates Architects

Emphasize the drama of an architecturally exciting space with monochromatic walls, floors, and furnishings in a restful cream color. Unobtrusive lighting fixtures on walls and ceiling help keep the look spare.

Photo: Kenneth Rice
Lighting Design: Catherine Ng, IES, and Randall Whitehead, IALD, ASID Affiliate
Design: Lawrence Masnada

In a living room with traditional architecture, create an airy look with bare hardwood floors and contemporary, solid furnishings set away from the walls. Furnishings of deep hues are dramatic against the light-colored walls and ceiling. Place a sculptural occasional chair— in this case, one designed by Charles Rennie Mackintosh—in a corner to unify a large space.

Photo: Eric Roth
Design: Francoise Theise, Adesso

An open floor plan affords opportunity for minimal treatment with the careful placement of furniture. Choose a sofa with classic lines and a warm color for its inviting comfort. Dining furniture with austere lines adds utility and grace.

Photo: Luis Ferreira Alves
Architecture: Souto Moura

Achieve the appeal of an uncluttered look in a classic setting with bare hardwood floors. Choose pale tints of blue for upholstered pieces and a glass-topped coffee table to reflect the serene tone.

Photo: Courtesy of Cassina USA

In a space as open and airy as this one, minimalist decorative treatment allows the architecture to prevail. Go monochromatic with all whites and add glass furnishings to express harmony and comfort.

Photo: Deborah Mazzoleni
Design: Rita St. Clair

Keep to the basics with monochromatic, light colors for
floors, walls, and furnishings. Furniture should be long
and low. Accessorize within the color range.

Photo: Courtesy of Cassina USA

Reflect the style of a post-modern fireplace wall in
furniture of like color and line. The result is a pleasing
unity of style and spirit.

Photo: Tim Street-Porter
Design: Barbara Barry

The contained lines of built-in seating allow the use of decorative pillows without resulting in a cluttered look. Coordinate fabrics in subtle tones to create visual continuity.

Photo: Russell Abraham
Design: Swatt Architects

Create a cozy atmosphere while keeping the look spare.

Here, the simple curves of the furnishings, in accord

with the lines of the room, create unity.

Photo: ©Norman McGrath
Architecture: Gwathmey Siegel and Associates Architects

The scenic view provides color and pattern through

floor-to-ceiling windows in this 1960s house designed

by Richard Neutra. Choose appealing contemporary

furniture for warmth.

Photo: Tim Street-Porter
Design: John Solomon
Furniture Design: George Nelson, Eero Saarinen, Charles and Ray Eames, and Mies van der Rohe

For a harmonious look, arrange seating to repeat

the symmetry of a wall of French doors. Use light

upholstery and sculptural accessories for added impact.

Photo: John Murdock
Architecture: Lee F. Mindel, AIA

Use bold splashes of color in furnishings with clean lines to enliven the mood without disturbing the streamlined style of a sleek living space. The absence of window and floor treatments draws attention to the utility and function of these essential elements.

Photo: Courtesy of Knoll

Take inspiration from the calla lily when selecting a sofa

to fill your picture window. Cream tones emphasize the

drama of this pared-down look.

Photo: Adrianne DePolo
Design: Joan Halperin Interior Design

dining rooms

Evoke the quintessentially minimalist Japanese

aesthetic with a low table and a display of fine ceramics.

A sculptural halogen wire system fills the room with

light without adding mass.

Photo: Russell Abraham
Lighting and Design: Donald Maxcy, ASID

Conceal both accent lighting and ambient lighting in a

ceiling soffit. Its spare lines complement the long,

highly polished dining table.

Photo: Russell Abraham
Lighting Design: Michael Souter, ASID

In an open floor plan, create visual interest in the dining

area with a table and chairs of contemporary design.

Hang a light fixture that follows the dimensions of the

table to help define the space. Lean framed paintings

against the wall to keep the look casual.

Photo: Tom Bonner
Architecture: Central Office of Architecture Partners

Use a shoji-like lighting fixture to illuminate a table

and chairs of dramatic wood for a subdued look with

Asian overtones. Allow the simplicity and grace of

the furniture to speak for itself.

Photo, Lighting, and Design: Courtesy of Lightolier

Furnish a dramatic dining alcove with a sleek table surrounded by complementary antique Chinese chairs to achieve an understated look. Match the lines in the chandelier with those of the table, and coordinate wall, window, and floor treatments in light wood tones to unify the effect.

Photo: Mario Ruiz
Interior, Table, and Chandelier Design: Mark Zeff

A quiet color palette of blush pink and soft gray pro-

vides a serene setting for contemporary dining furniture

in deep tones. Exposed hardwood floors and a lighting

fixture of spare design maintain the uncluttered look.

Photo: Salvatore M. Lovinello
Design: David A. Seglin, HSP/Ltd., Seglin Associates

Unify a spacious room with understated style. Here, undressed windows serve as a backdrop for the large dining table lined with companion chairs. (These Hoffman chairs were commissioned by ICF.)

Photo: Richard Richenbach
Design: David Webster and Associates

Keep a tiny dining area uncluttered by using a glass-topped pedestal table and high-backed chairs with solid, clean lines. Light the deck beyond to give the room a more spacious feeling.

Photo: Ben Jankin

Lighting Design: Catherine Ng, IES, and Randall Whitehead, IALD, ASID Affiliate

Design: Christian Wright and Gerald Simpkins

In a house built to maximize the view, minimal interiors heighten the panoramic effect. Use simple lines and cue the color palette to the scenery beyond the window for perfect harmony.

Photo: Charley Daniels
Architecture: Ron Goldman, FAIA; Bob Firth, AIA; and Clelio Boccato, AIA
Design: James Kwan

Choose a glass fixture with clean lines and Art Deco

flair to concentrate attention on highly polished dining

furniture. The multiple textures of the floral arrangement

constitute the single elaborate element in the room.

Photo, Lighting Design, Interior Design: Courtesy of Lightolier

In a casual dining area, opt for banquette seating to provide ample capacity with pared-down style.

Photo: Tim Street-Porter
Design: Mark Mack Architects

Use a restful pale gray to set the tone in a peaceful dining room that is adorned mainly with lighting and mirrors. Allow accessories to stand out by virtue of their simplicity and arresting presentation.

Photo and Lighting Design: Randall Whitehead
Design: Christian Wright and Gerald Simpkins

Achieve an extreme minimalist look with transparent furnishings. Here, a glass tabletop on a glass base is surrounded by light-colored chairs. The lighting fixtures and glass-block wall combine with the green of the floor to create a luminous dining room.

Photo: Tim Street-Porter
Design: Brian Murphy Architects

Repeat the line of your dining table in a suspended ceiling detail to create a harmonious look while providing housing for accent and ambient lighting. A monochromatic color scheme unites the space.

Photo: Kenneth Rice
Lighting Design: Catherine Ng and Randall Whitehead
Design: Lawrence Masnada
Architecture: Sid Del Mar Leach

An unadorned dining area can be a backdrop for any

table setting. Use glass-topped tables and simple chairs

that work in either casual or formal treatments.

Photo: Courtesy of B&B Italia
Table Design: Paolo Piva for B&B Italia

For a spare, contemporary look, surround a stylish

table (this one designed by Le Corbusier) with folding

French garden chairs. The effect is at once whimsical

and dramatic.

Photo: Eric Roth
Design: Veronique Louvet

In a loft dining area, place a glass-topped table on

a gridded base to echo the structural lines of the

architecture. Match wooden chairs to the hardwood

floor for further unity.

Photo: Salvatore Lovinello
Design: David A. Seglin, HSP/Ltd., Seglin Associates

Create interest in a simply appointed dining area by
placing the table at an angle in the room. The resulting
air of informality suits the variation in the chair finishes
and cut-out details.

Photo: Tim Street-Porter
Design: Frank Israel

kitchens

Provide a smooth, uncluttered backdrop for art in

the kitchen with flat-panel cabinet doors and hidden

hardware. A monochromatic color scheme and recessed

lighting maximize the effect.

Photo: Russell Abraham
Lighting and Design: Donald Maxcy, ASID

Provide an unobstructed view of a kitchen with a

sleek, compact range hood, heightening the impact

of the total design.

Photo and Design: Technical Office of Alberticasador

For a clean look, replace kitchen cabinet doors with

etched glass. The etching hides the contents of the

cabinets, while the glass opens up the room.

Photo: Robert Perron

This kitchen achieves a warm atmosphere with earthy

grays. Sunlight reflecting off gleaming stainless-steel

surfaces becomes a golden glow. Spare lines and

recessed lighting keep the look clean and functional.

Photo: Hedrich Blessing Ltd.
Design: Rand Elliott, FAIA

Create interest and harmony in the kitchen by repeating

the curved line of a soffit in the counters. An appealing

tone-on-tone color scheme with complementary slate

countertop is restful and inviting.

Photo: Alan Weintraub

Use subtle values of gray in a monochromatic kitchen

for a spare look. Lighting with halogens suspended

from wire is both minimalist and practical.

Photo: Alan Weintraub

Flat-front cabinets and concealed hardware make for a
clean look in the kitchen. Monochromatic grays of varying textures add interest. A built-in wine rack of the
simplest design marries function with form.

Photo: Hedrich Blessing Ltd.
Design: Rand Elliott, FAIA

Achieve a restful, uncluttered look with oyster-white walls and cabinets and polished granite counters. Frosted glass in wall cabinets lightens the space and adds interest with abstract shapes created by the tableware within.

Design: Leslie Jones, Inc.

Opt for a proportional oval island in a long, narrow kitchen. Top it with an oval range hood for a harmonious, spare look.

Photo: Russell Abraham
Design: Greg Smith

Continue the low-key look of the kitchen in a breakfast nook with a glass-topped table, sleek chairs, and a simple light fixture. Warm the spot with a touch of orange.

Photo: Robert Ricciardelli
Design: John Berenson

Use stainless-steel appliances, counters, and cabinets to generate a utilitarian, industrial look. Here, a glass-block window magnifies the ambient light, emphasizing the sheen of the steel.

Photo: Tim Street-Porter
Design: Antoine Kripacz

Create a sophisticated, cosmopolitan ambiance using

extreme colors—black walls offset by a red accent

wall—combined with smooth stainless-steel appliances.

Use unobtrusive furnishings with clean lines for dramatic

appeal.

Photo: Phillip Ennis
Design: Vogel-Mulea

In an expansive contemporary kitchen, achieve a spare look by installing a large center island generously for food preparation and casual dining. The simple lines of the black stools are echoed in the pendant lighting. Sleek surfaces complete the effect.

Photo: Bill Rothschild
Design: Robert Madey, AIA

Emphasize an oval island using low-voltage, stemmed fixtures to bounce light off the polished marble counter. Sleek surfaces and a monochromatic color scheme provide an understated backdrop for this dramatic effect.

Photo: Eric Zepeda
Design: Charles J. Grebmeier and Gunnar Burklund

In a small kitchen with warm wood tones, substituting a stainless-steel table for a center island adds flexibility. Match the material to the appliances to lighten the effect of the heavy wood.

Photo: Tim Street-Porter

Illuminate a center island with pendant lighting fixtures, dramatically hung. Maintain a clean look while softening the strong lines of the lights, cabinet doors, and window shades with curves in the island's countertop and the range hood.

Photo: Alan Weintraub
Lighting Design: Catherine Ng and Randall Whitehead
Design: Vicky Doubleday and Peter Gutkin

Open up a small kitchen by creating a sweeping arch to divide it from the adjacent room. Keep surfaces and lines simple and use light colors to brighten and enlarge the area.

Photo: John Kane
Design: McKee Patterson, Austin Patterson Disston Architects

bedrooms

The plain lines of this large doorway frame a master bedroom. Spare furnishings, placed symmetrically within the space, declare the room's function. Light fabrics on the bed coordinate with the walls and offset the sophisticated dark-wood floor.

Photo: Luis Ferreira Alves
Architecture: Eduardo Souto Moura

Attain a spare look in a bedroom of industrial design with furnishings that are part of the structure. A headboard that serves as a dividing wall can provide a platform for the bed and side tables. Soften the effect of steel and hard edges with a sheared-fur bedspread.

Photo: Tim Street-Porter
Design: Augustin Hernandez

Embed your mattress in a carpeted surround, a continuation of the carpeted floor, for unity. Add color with a spectrum art light to keep the room from feeling stark.

Photo: Norman McGrath

Conceal clothing and accessories behind flat-paneled

folding doors to eliminate clutter. Here, the warm

rose tone of the doors is echoed in the headboard,

reinforcing the single identity of the space.

Photo: Wardrobe by B&B Italia
Design: Studio Kairos

Focus attention on function with clean-lined, lacquered

furniture. Here, black balances the dark wood of the

ceiling and the oyster-white walls and carpet.

Contemporary lighting keeps the look trim.

Photo: Richard Mandelkorn

Use structural idiosyncrasies to advantage by
incorporating them into the furnishings. Here, the posts
become an extension of the headboard when draped
with coordinating fabric, creating a cohesive look.

Photo: Bedroom by Ligne Roset

Let flat-paneled closet doors in bold blue set the theme
in a bedroom. A translucent headboard provides interest
without visual obstruction. The uninterrupted curves of
the clever side-table arm and contemporary lamp seal
the minimal look.

Photo: Courtesy of B&B Italia
Design: Bedroom by B&B Italia

Make the focal point an oversized decorative mirror in an otherwise unadorned bedroom. A monochromatic palette and restrained textures provide a serene backdrop.

Photo: Eric Roth
Design: Veronique Louvet

Create a private corner in a bedroom. Surround a simple, light-colored chair with sheer drapery, hung double.

Photo: Courtesy of Imperial Wallcoverings

A pallet suspended by wires from the ceiling serves as a bed. To accentuate the room's place in the technological era, an overhead video camera and screen record the sleeper's experience. This is the epitome of minimalism.

Photo: Norman McGrath, courtesy of American Hospital of Paris French Designers Showhouse
Design: Jane Victor and Jennifer Ellenberg, Jane Victor Associates

Maintain clean lines with continuity of form. Here, a four-poster bed with Asian overtones complements the windows in a similar style and wood. The large rectangular openings are consistent with the open feel of the space.

Photo: Paul Rocheleau, courtesy of Thos. Moser Cabinetmakers

In a monochromatic bedroom, underscore the focal importance of the bed with an unusual architectural treatment. Here, stepped and curved lacquered panels are downlit from recessed fixtures to highlight their horizontal lines.

Photo: Phillip Ennis
Design: Vince Lattuca

Choose a bed with simple lines for a guest room. This upholstered, wingback headboard provides sufficient decorative impact to complete the low-key decor, with a simple side table for utility.

Photo: Courtesy of Cassina USA

In a country bedroom, achieve a minimal look with a small area rug set on gleaming hardwood floors. Select furniture with refined lines, such as this pencil-post bed in warm cherry wood.

Photo: Paul Rocheleau, courtesy of Thos. Moser Cabinetmakers

Use soft cushions on a built-in window seat for an inviting reading space. A monochromatic color scheme keeps the look spare. Use Mecho window shades to filter the sunlight.

Photo: Tim Street-Porter
Design: Lenny Steinberg

I waited on the corner for my blind date. When this girl walked by, I said, "Are you Linda?" She said, "Are you Richard?" I said "Yeah." She said, "I'm not Linda."

Create artistic interest on a white wall with minimalist presentation of a witty anecdote. A spread of hearty fabric adds warm appeal.

Photo: Tim Street-Porter
Design: Daniel Sachs

In a bedroom with a wall of windows, allow light to filter through sheer drapery to create an ephemeral atmosphere. Choose headboard, table, and chairs with clean lines and center the bed in the room for added appeal.

Photo: Paul Warchol
Design: Peter L. Gluck and Partners, Architects

The minimalist approach does not preclude the excitement of bold color. Keep the palette monochromatic while varying values and chroma from dark to bright. Maintain clarity of style with spare furnishings.

Photo: Bedroom by Cassina USA

bathrooms

In a large, sunny bathroom, emphasize the gleaming white of tiles and fixtures with wallpaper and borders colored with the faintest touch of blue. A white chair covered in crisp cotton adds function without detracting from the purity of the look.

Photo: Courtesy of Imperial Wallcoverings

Use varied materials to enliven spare interiors. Blown-glass sconces over a polished granite counter, glass knobs, and a variegated mosaic tile wall add glow, shine, and pattern to this small bathroom.

Photo: Ira Montgomery
Lighting Design: Barbara Bouyea, IALD, IES
Design and Architecture: Mil Bodron

Suspend a round mirror over a sleek, curved vanity in a small bathroom. A wall sconce of simple lines provides task lighting.

Photo: Douglas A. Salin
Lighting Design: Catherine Ng, IES and Randall Whitehead, IALD, ASID Affiliate,
Design: Helen C. Reuter

The exclusive use of white marble for walls, floors, and sinks creates a pristine bath. Stainless-steel frames for mirrors and shower doors seal the spa-like effect.

Photo: Luis Ferreira Alves
Architecture: Eduardo Souto Moura

Create a seamless, open effect with flat, clear-glass

shower doors. Lighting along the ceiling at the inside

wall makes this unadorned bathroom glow.

Photo: Ira Montgomery
Lighting Design: Barbara Bouyea, IALD, IES
Design: Allen Kirsch

Choose neutral tones and shiny surfaces for a small

bath. Oversized mirrors appear to expand the space, and

dual sinks actually expand its utility. Spare accessories

add interest without clutter.

Design: Leslie Jones, Inc.

For a spare yet sparkling bathroom, form a room divider with translucent glass blocks. Glass countertops and gleaming stainless basins complete the effect.

Photo: Russell Abraham
Lighting Design and Architecture: Dan Frederick

Use like textures to provide continuity when a contrasting color scheme is employed. Shiny navy-blue tiles, when surrounded by large areas of equally shiny pure white, act as a resting place for the eye.

Photo: Phillip Ennis
Design: Ultimate Sound Installations, Inc.

In an ocean-front home, optimize the limitless seascape with understated interior spaces. Glass walls for the bath provide unobstructed views, which are all the adornment necessary in this spectacular setting.

Photo: Russell Shubin
Architecture: Russell Shubin, AIA, and Timothy Morgan Steele

Use clean lines and sleek surfaces to make the bath a place of relaxation. Here, the monochromatic floor and walls are accented only by the gray veins in the marble, echoed in the black-and-white photography on the wall.

Photo: Hedrich Blessing Ltd.
Design: Floyd Anderson

In a large bathroom, create texture by using
pinpoint spots of contrasting color in an otherwise
monochromatic color scheme. The effect is dramatic
while the look is minimal.

Photo: Phillip Ennis
Design: Vogel-Mulea

Make your master suite cohesive with a large doorway to the bath and pocket doors for a clean, wide-open look. Continue the bedroom flooring across the threshold for unity. Spare bath fixtures in luxurious materials convey a sophisticated sensibility.

Photo: Luis Ferreira Alves
Architecture: Eduardo Souto Moura

For a serene setting, use warm, earthy surfaces polished to reflect the light from recessed fixtures.

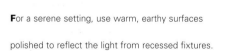

Photo: Gil Edelstein
Lighting Design: Linda Ferry
Design: John Schneider

Set a minimalist tone with glass sinks. Enhance their

sculptural quality with lighting. Vanities with spare lines

in a glowing monochromatic color scheme complete

the effect.

Photo: www.davidduncanlivingston.com
Lighting Design: Jim Gillam
Design: Maria Fisher

outdoor rooms
and patios

Give a rustic screened porch the minimal treatment

with essential furnishings of evocative design, creating

interest without excess.

Photo: David Lake
Architecture: David Lake and Ted Flato

For clean, cool treatment of a beachfront patio, use

austere white furniture. French limestone paving tiles

blend with the sandy dunes beyond.

Photo: Tim Street-Porter
Architecture: Arthur Erickson
Design: Barbara Barry

On a small deck with a spectacular panorama,

proportionate furniture of unassuming line and texture

serves its purpose without creating a distraction.

Substitute a glass panel for a portion of the wall to

maximize the view.

Photo and Architecture: David Hertz, AIA

A central courtyard allows for private outdoor living

space in a congested area. Use green Vermont slate

paving for weatherproof flooring with spa-like appeal.

An unadorned contemporary fountain adds sculptural

interest.

Photo: Grey Crawford
Architecture: Anne Troutman

An industrial-look screened porch can become a dining

area on a grand scale while maintaining its simple

appeal. Surround a large, heavy wood table with simple

chairs. Add a sideboard for utility.

Photo: Undine Pröhl
Architecture: David Lake and Ted Flato

directory of designers

Floyd Anderson
Lohan Associates
225 N. Michigan Avenue
Chicago, IL 60601

Alberticasador S.R.L.
Corso Como, 46
20051 Limbiate (MI) ITALY

Austin Patterson Disston Architects
376 Pequot Avenue
P.O. Box 61
Southport, CT 06490

B&B Italia, USA, Inc.
150 East 58th Street
Architects and Designers Building
New York, NY 10155

Barbara Barry
Barbara Barry Incorporated
526 Pico Boulevard
Los Angeles, CA 90035

John Berenson, ASID
John Berenson Interior Design
180 N.E. 39th St., Suite 220
Miami, FL 33137

Mil Bodron Design
2801 West Lemmon Avenue
Suite 201
Dallas, TX 75204

Barbara Bouyea, IALD, IES
Bouyea & Associates
3811 Turtle Creek Boulevard, Suite 1010
Dallas, TX 75219

Cassina USA
200 McKay Road
Huntington Station, NY 11746

Ron Golan, Eric A. Kahn, Russell N. Thomsen
Central Office of Architecture
1056 S. Sierra Bonita Avenue
Los Angeles, CA 90019-2571

Michael C.F. Chan & Associates, Inc.
3550 W. 6th Street, PH
Los Angeles, CA 90020

Celeste Cooper, ASID
Repetoire
560 Harrison Avenue
Boston, MA 02118

Wally Cunningham, Architect
1102 West Arbor Drive
San Diego, CA 92103

Damga Design
207 East 76th Street, #2D
New York, NY 10021

Steven Ehrlich Architects
2210 Colorado Avenue
Santa Monica, CA 90404

Rand Elliott, FAIA
Elliott & Associates Architects
35 Harrison Avenue
Oklahoma City, OK 73104

Linda Ferry IESNA, ASID (affiliate)
Architectural Illumination
P.O. Box 2690
Monterey, CA 93942

James Gillam Architects
1841 Powell Street
San Francisco, CA 94133

Peter L. Gluck and Partners, Architects
19 Union Square West, 12th floor
New York, NY 10003

Ron Goldman, FAIA
Bob Firth, AIA
Clelio Boccato, AIA
Goldman Firth Boccato Architects
24955 Pacific Coast Highway, Suite A202
Malibu, CA 90265

Charles J.Grebmeier
Gunnar Burklund
Grebmeier Burklund
1298 Sacramento Street
San Francisco, CA 94108

Charles Paxton Gremillion
Loyd-Paxton Inc.
3636 Maple Avenue
Dallas, TX 75219

Charles Gwathmey
Robert Siegel
Gwathmey Siegel
475 Tenth Avenue
New York, NY 10018

Joan Halperin
401 E. 80th Street
New York, NY 10021

Augustin Hernandez
Bosques De Acasias 61
Mexico City, Mexico 11700

David Hertz, AIA
Syndesis
2908 Colorado Avenue
Santa Monica, CA 90404

Imperial Wallcoverings
23645 Mercantile Road
Beechwood, OH 44122

Frank Israel
254 South Robertson
Los Angeles, CA 90211

Leslie Jones, Inc.
754 N. Milwaukee Avenue
Chicago, IL 60622

Alberto Kalach
Daniel Alvarez
Kalach + Alvarez
Atlanta 143, Co. Nochebuena
03720, Mexico D.F.
Mexico

Kentucky Wood Floors
P.O. Box 33276
Louisville, KY 40232

Allen Kirsch Interior Design
3131 Turtle Creek Boulevard, Suite 820
Dallas, TX 75219

Knoll
1235 Water Street
East Greenville, PA 18041

James Kwan
Kwan Design
409 North Lucerne Boulevard
Los Angeles, CA 90004

David Lake
Ted Flato
Lake & Flato Inc.
311 Third Street
Suite 200
San Antonio, TX 78205

Vince Lattuca
c/o Visconti & Co.
245 East 57th Street
New York, NY 10021

Sid Del Mar Leach, ASID
Classic Design Associates
288 Butterfield Road
San Anselmo, CA 94960

Lightolier
631 Airport Road
Fall River, MA 02720
Ligne Roset
Roset USA Corporation
200 Lexington Avenue
New York, NY 10016

Veronique Louvet
140 Campbell Street
Roxbury, MA 02119

Mark Mack Architects
246 First Street
San Francisco, CA 94103

Robert Madey, AIA, Architect
1175 Montauk Highway
West Islip, NY 11795

Lawrence Masnada
Lawrence Masnada Design
1745 20th Street
San Francisco, CA 94207

Donald Maxcy, ASID
Maxcy Design
Lincoln between 7th & 8th
P.O. Box 5507
Carmel, CA 93921

Lee F. Mindel, AIA
Shelton, Mindel & Associates
216 West 18th Street
New York, NY 10011

Thos. Moser Cabinetmakers
72 Wright's Landing
P.O. Box 1237
Auburn, ME 04211

Brian Murphy Architects
147 West Channel Road
Santa Monica, CA 90402

Catherine Ng, IES
Light Source Design Group
1246 18th Street
San Francisco, CA 94107

Guinter Parschalk
RDX-Radix Commercial Ltda
Rua Fernando Falcao, 121
Sao Paulo, Sao Paulo
03180-001 Brazil

Dan Phipps and Associates
131 Post Street
San Francisco, CA 94109

Helen C. Reuter
Details, Inc.
1250 Jones Street, #1102
San Francisco, CA 94109

Craig A. Roeder & Associates
3829 North Hall Street
Dallas, TX 75219

Daniel Sachs
10 Greene Street
New York, NY 10013

Rita St. Clair
Rita St. Clair Associates, Inc.
1009 N. Charles Street
Baltimore, MD 21201

John Schneider Design
P.O. Box 1457
Pebble Beach, CA 93953

Josh Schweitzer
Schweitzer BIM
5543 West Washington Boulevard
Los Angeles, CA 90016

David A. Seglin, AIA
HSP/Ltd., Seglin Associates
430 W. Erie, #510
Chicago, IL 60610

Russell Shubin, AIA
Shubin + Donaldson Architects
629 State Street, Suite 242
Santa Barbara, CA 93101

David Allen Smith Architect
444 Pearl Street, Suite B2
Monterey, CA 93940

Michael Souter, ASID
Louminae Souter
1740 Army Street, 2nd Floor
San Francisco, CA 94124

Eduardo Souto de Moura
Souto Moura - Arquitectos, Lda.
Rua do Aleixo, 53
4150 Porto
Portugal

Lenny Steinberg
2517 Ocean Front Walk
Venice, CA 90291

Candida Tabet
Mantovani & Tabet Com. De Moveis Ltda
Rua Medeiros de Albuquerque, 23
Sao Paulo, Sao Paulo
05436-060 Brazil

Loyd Ray Taylor
Loyd-Paxton Inc
3636 Maple Avenue
Dallas, TX 75219

Francoise Theise
Adesso
200 Boylston Street
Boston, MA 02116

Anne Troutman
Troutman & Associates
1721 Pier Avenue
Santa Monica, CA 90405

Ultimate Sound Installations, Inc.
36-16 29th Street
Long Island City, NY 11106

Jane Victor
Jennifer Ellenberg
Jane Victor Associates
34 West Ninth Street
New York, NY 10011

David Webster & Associates
254 West 25th Street
New York, NY 10001

Randall Whitehead, IALD, Principal
Light Source
1210 18th Street
San Francisco, CA 94107

Christian Wright
Robert Hering & Associates
151 Vermont Street, #7
San Francisco, CA 94103

Mark Zeff Consulting Group Inc.
260 W. 72nd Street, Suite 12B
New York, NY 10023

index